A Ghost in the Water

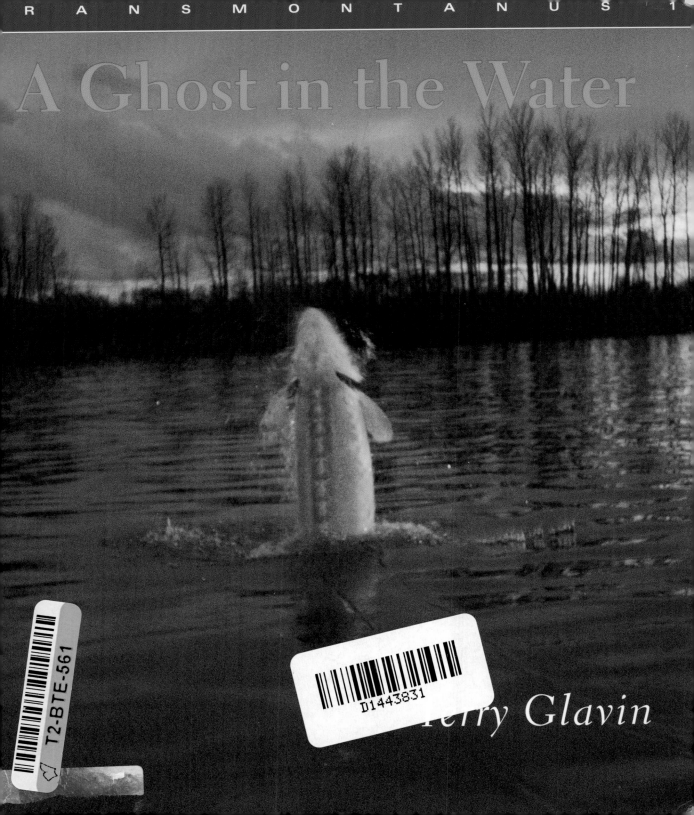

Terry Glavin

A Ghost in the Water

TRANSMONTANUS 1

Published by New Star Books

Series Editor: Terry Glavin

A Ghost

in the Water

Terry Glavin

TRANSMONTANUS / **NEW STAR BOOKS** VANCOUVER

CONTENTS

Dark nights are chosen,

when the fish, swimming along through the salt water,

reveals its presence by a phosphorescent light

surrounding the body.

— "Lex," the correspondent's pseudonym, describing
Acipenser transmontanus in Semiahmoo Bay
in the May 28, 1894, edition of the New Westminster
Columbian newspaper.

I

CLOTHED-WITH-POWER'S DAUGHTER

The snow is gone now, even from the highest mountains to the north, from Slollicum Peak to Dog Mountain, and all along the top of the southern wall of the Lillooet Range. Far above the alpine, the mountain peaks have become blue in the heat of summer. Circling in a wide arc to the east and to the south, all the mountain peaks are bare and stark against the summer sky. Earlier in the day, the peak of Mount Slesse, rising up behind Mount MacFarlane, had become a black dagger in the sky above Mount Tamihi, the Place of the Deformed, and above all the other mountains of the Skagit Range that fall away behind Mount Cheam. ¶ From the north, Mount Cheam is the mother who was transformed with her daughters and her dog after leaving her husband, and now he is Mount Baker, in the Cascades. From the east, Cheam's heights are four sisters, and it is the youngest who stands in front. At the time of the Great Flood, she is said to have wept at what had become of the people below. Her tears become Bridal Falls. They scatter into a creek that joins the Fraser River at a point just upstream and around a wooded bend from the place where we are anchored, in deep water, a stone's throw off the north bank in a small K&C runabout that rolls gently in the swells. It is 6:10 p.m., Tuesday, July 19, 1994. We are drinking Canterbury Dark out of cans. The river is hissing.

Marvin Rosenau and I have the canopy for shade, but there is less of it every minute because the sun is falling towards the river, which flows through the weir of these mountains into the horizon to the southwest and directly into the path of the slowly falling sun. I mark its descent by the knob on top of Mount Woodside and the hump of Mount Calamity on the north bank. Which will soon mean little shade at all, except what shadow falls behind Nick Basok, a big man with a camouflage baseball cap sitting an arm's length from three sturdy fishing rods propped against the sky on the transom.

The gear we are using includes 80-pound test line and size 10 hooks, held at the bottom with 14-ounce weights, which should be enough to secure the animal that brought us here, if there are any down there, alive, at the bottom of the river, and if we actually catch one. It is known in the scientific literature as *Acipenser transmontanus*, a giant freshwater creature that emerged in the Upper Cretaceous period of the Mesozoic era and somehow survived the great extinctions of the ages. It is the largest freshwater fish in North America. It is known locally as the Fraser River white sturgeon.

Nick Basok grew up in Chilliwack. He has been fishing since he was 10. He would fish all summer and take a bucket of worms and go down to Gill Road and catch chub in the fall, when nothing else was going on. He has spent as much time on the river as his life has been able to afford him. He is 45 now. He is a fish culturist at the Fraser Valley Trout Hatchery in Sumas. For him, if this had a beginning at all, it was three decades ago. He caught his first sturgeon when he was 14 years old, with his grandfather, on a sandbar near Fergie's place at the mouth of the Harrison River. They were using worms on a handline.

The fish he caught was more than two feet long. They let it go.

The first time Marvin caught a sturgeon, it was with what he now describes as a primitive bar rig, using worms. It was at the old dock at Fraser Mills, just below the mouth of the Coquitlam River. He was 14. He didn't have a ruler with him but he had a two-dollar bill, and end over end at six inches a length he figured it was about a yard long. He took it home and his mother made fish and chips. He still remembers it as the nicest fish he has ever caught in his life. He's 38 now. He is the provincial government's chief sturgeon biologist.

Like Rosenau and Basok, I grew up within shouting distance of this river. I had never found a sturgeon of any size on the end of any line I ever cast, but I was dimly aware of the rumours. Giant, 20-foot water monsters dwelt in the depths of the river. They fell within a childhood taxonomy that included the Sasquatch, the ghosts that haunted the house on Russell Avenue, terrifying swamp animals from the Burnaby flats and the creatures that lurked in long-forgotten tunnels under the streets of New Westminster. If rumours of the water creature had some credible origin, it may have been this report, in the August 14, 1897, edition of the New Westminster *Columbian*:

Several very large ones have been caught in the Fraser, one over 1,800 lbs. being reported. The largest of which any authenticated record has been kept was one weighing 1,387 lbs., which was caught opposite this city in the early days by one of W.H. Vianen's fishermen. Governor Seymour and the others were at the wharf when it was landed from the boat, and they sent it to Victoria where it created quite a furor. Soon after this, one weighing 1,200 lbs. was taken, and a year or two ago, one over 1,100 lbs. was taken up to the exhibition grounds during the fair. Only this week, several 600 pounders were caught, while from 400 lbs. down is a daily occurrence.

For me, it began in 1981 when I met Carl Leon, who told me about sturgeon and about what the old people used to say.

Leon is dead now, but back then he was a formidable man, a logger in a John Deere baseball cap, the chief of the Katzie Indian band at the foot of Bonson Road in Pitt Meadows. A hiker had just come out of the mountains above Pitt Lake with a bag full of bones he said he found at the entrance to a cave.

There was a slab of rock blocking the cave entrance. The bones were underneath it. The bones turned out to be from four people, along with some charred bones of animals and birds, and the discovery brought back old stories Leon vaguely remembered about a strange tribe of cliff-dwellers who lived in a remote, high valley with a single, narrow passageway that could be entered for only a few weeks every year because of the deep snow.

The old people on the reserve used to tell stories about these people. Small, shy people. They used to leave paintings on rock walls.

And it got Carl thinking about Thunderbird Hole, a cave halfway up a sheer wall of rock above the east bank of Pitt Lake, about halfway to the top of the lake. In the Katzie tradition, the Thunderbird arose from its sleep there to soar over the world.

Carl listened to these stories when he was a boy, and on weekends he'd head up to the lake with his friends, but it was useless trying to climb to the cave. They fired their rifles at the mouth of the cave. Hawks flew out of it.

There was a local farmhand, a Swiss with climbing gear from the old country. Carl and his friends pursuaded him to climb to the top, behind the rock face, and lower rope down so they could climb up. But the farmhand fell, and the way Carl remembered it he went a little crazy and came at them in their canoe with a knife.

As the years passed, the top of a giant fir tree at the base of the cliff was growing close to Thunderbird Hole, and Carl climbed it once, but from where he clung to the fir's upper limbs it was still too far to see inside the cave. More years passed. He asked a friend with a pilot's licence to fly close to it. He could see inside. It wasn't deep. But they flew by too quickly to make out much. He always wanted to try it again, but something always got in the way.

Carl told me about Thunderbird Hole in 1981. We were sitting in his run-down office. I asked him what he knew about the stories of giant fish in the river. He put the bones from the cave back in a drawer. He said it was too bad Old Pierre wasn't still around. Old Pierre knew sturgeon stories.

Carl died two years ago. He never did learn for certain who those cave people might have been, but he was convinced they were not among the Katzie's ancestors. The Katzie had always been quite certain about who their ancestors were, and in 1936, Old Pierre, one of the great Coast Salish medicine people of his generation, recounted the Katzie genesis stories to anthropologist Diamond Jenness. Although Old Pierre was 75 at the time, he provided a lucid and precise articulation of the Katzie view of events that occurred at the beginning of time, and how sturgeon were intimately involved in these events. At the beginning of the world, God placed people at different places, and the Katzie descended from the first people God created at Pitt Lake, whose ruler was known as Clothed-With-Power. This first chief had a daughter and a son. The girl spent all her days swimming, and because of this she was transformed into a sturgeon, the first fish to inhabit Pitt Lake, and it was from this girl that all the sturgeon of the Fraser River descended. After she was changed, her brother wept inconsolably, so Clothed-With-Power took the silk-like hair of a mountain goat, laid it on the boy's head and arms, and transformed him into a white owl-like bird that could be seen only by Clothed-With-Power's descendants. It is only by human hand that a sturgeon can die, and those that wish to take a sturgeon would first seek spirit power from this white bird. Sometimes, the sturgeon might avail itself directly to a fisherman, Old Pierre told Jenness. In the case of one spirit dancer, Old Pierre said:

When he danced and chanted his sturgeon song, a column of steam streamed from his body as if from a kettle. He once announced, as he ended his dance, "Three girls have come in," and the next morning he went out and caught exactly three sturgeon.

In 1950, Chilliwack elder Robert Joe, who was 68 at the time, told anthropologist Wilson Duff about the siwil, which Duff translates as "the magical utterance." It was a particular kind of incantation, in a strange language that no one could speak anymore. The siwil is inheritable, and although it could be put to many uses, Robert Joe remembered fishing once with his grandfather's brother, who caught a sturgeon that fought long and hard and would not give up. The old man started singing his siwil song, and the sturgeon floated to the surface, belly up.

But Marvin, Nick and I are resigned to settle for chance, and this place below Mount Cheam and this hot summer night, and the more utilitarian contents of Nick's bait box, from which he had taken what he calls "garlic eels," meaning lampreys. A piece of a big one, more than a foot long, and some smaller ones. Marvin had sprayed WD 40 into the mouths of two small eels he used to bait his hook. Something about the smell of oil. Nick had spun a chunk of chinook roe onto the third hook, from a 22-pounder he caught the night before, and he cast all three hard — off the port side, the starboard side and straight downstream.

And so we watch the rod tips for any movement, any communication telegraphed along the lines from the bottom of the river. The sun continues its slow descent through the bright blue sky. In the distance, there is the faint hum of truck traffic on the 401. There is a distant clatter from the few anglers packing it in over at Rosedale Bar. A skein of Canada geese unfurls across the river from the heavy stand of cottonwood that blankets Ferry Island, the boat rocks drowsily and we settle in. We open three more cans of Canterbury Dark. We wait.

II

MUCH DAMAGED
ON THE VOYAGE

The events that brought us together on the river began on Monday, September 13, 1993. A call came through to Rosenau's cubbyhole of an office on the third floor of the provincial environment ministry's regional offices in Surrey, where he had been working ever since he had come home with a PhD from the University of Waikato in New Zealand in 1990. He had been labouring away on a handful of portfolios that nobody else really wanted. Things like crayfish, sturgeon, the endangered Salish sucker, the Cultus Lake sculpin and the Nooksack dace. He was trying his best to maintain within the bureaucracy and the realm of public policy at least a modicum of scientific interest in these rather unglamorous fish when Annie Van den Berg called from her home at Derby Reach, on the Fraser River near Fort Langley. Something hideous and strange had washed up on the riverbank, in her own backyard, and she wasn't quite sure what it was. ¶ It sounded like a Fraser River white sturgeon, one of those rare old giants that still show up from time to time. Rosenau noted the details and made plans to head out in a day or two

FACING PAGE: *"Harbourmaster Brown," Leif Wike of the Westminster Fish Company, and an unidentified third man with a giant Fraser River white sturgeon caught in the 1950s.* WESTMINSTER FISH COMPANY

to cut it up and have the lab look at the pieces. It turned out to be a real old-timer, probably 100 years old or older. Maybe it got caught in an Indian gillnet and died. Maybe it was just old, and died of a heart attack. He didn't think much of it at first. Just an obscure creature from the past, a holdover from another age, dead on a sandbar in Langley. These things happen.

In the sprawling suburban landscape that has covered most of the lower Fraser's side channels and sloughs since World War II, few people were aware that such a creature had once thrived here. After a few years in the late 1800s, when the river was all but emptied of them, the giant Fraser River white sturgeon seem to just vanish from memory, perhaps emerging now and again in a darker corner of the popular imagination, that place inhabited by sea serpents and dragons, a place where fish, being always below the surface of water, always unseen, so readily conjure the fanciful. And sometimes they pop up in one of the weekly newspapers in the valley. Local Man Catches Huge Fish.

But for the most part, they just vanish.

There was a remnant population still, but it had not been holding its own. They had been disappearing from their old haunts along the Fraser for some time, and "alarming trends" indicating what scientists call recruitment failure — the term that comes up often in any discussion of the East coast's northern cod stocks — were starting to show up in ministry reports. Still, there were studies underway and stricter conservation measures under review, and Rosenau was making headway with the commercial salmon fishermen who catch sturgeon by accident, and the few anglers who catch them for sport, and things had been starting to look up, if maintaining the relics of a near-extinct beast in an increasingly unfavourable environment could be described as a situation that was looking up. And it was hard work made no easier by the obscurity of the animal in the scientific literature. Biologists still don't know for certain where or how white sturgeon spawn, and they know just as little about its feeding patterns and migratory behaviour, and they know even less about how many are left. Rarely studied, rarely even seen. Half myth, like the fish that brings lost objects from the bottom of the sea or the fish that is half woman or the fish that swallows a man. For scientists, the problem with white sturgeon is that the line between fact and folklore is hard to find, and given what little is known to science about these fish, sometimes it's hard to say for certain whether a line exists at all. They become creatures of the imagination, turning up in places appropriate to such phenomena, like Diana Hartog's poetic bestiary:

Carl Campbell and Carman Johnston with a rare giant caught near Chilliwack in the 1950s.
CHILLIWACK MUSEUM AND HISTORICAL SOCIETY (P7528)

Rumours of sturgeon feed miles down, along the bottom of northern lakes. For this species, death is final and appears as a great blinding sun at which they gape, ascending, reeled up on shore by a team of horses.

But life is lived in the dark.

Twenty feet long and gunmetal grey, the sturgeon swim among schools of sunken locomotives — old steam engines which have flung themselves off the end of the line, to lie tilted on their sides, breathing deeply through their gills; they can't move, their single headlamps angle off with fixed stares into the watery murk.

The sturgeon glide through these beams . . .

The very existence of the white sturgeon as a separate species was not established with certainty until the 1830s, two decades after the fish made what was probably its first appearance in the written word, in the July 8, 1808, entry in the journal of the explorer Simon Fraser, the first white man to traverse the Sto:lo territory. He had just arrived at the Sto:los' upriver frontier with the Nlaka'pamux, at what is now Spuzzum. Making his way down through the Black Canyon enclosing Hell's Gate, Fraser's travel was slow and arduous, and his journal entries show an increasing frustration and surliness. He had been five years on the great journey to determine a route overland to the mouth of the Columbia River, and Fraser was beginning to fear that the river he had been following all along was not the Columbia at all, a suspicion that deepened as the river took a dramatic turn to the west. He began to see seals in the water, and the Natives kept insisting that the sea was not far away. And Fraser's party was several degrees of latitude north of the Columbia's mouth.

The river had turned clearly to westward. It was just below Hope, not far from the place where Rosenau, Basok and I are anchored in the river. It was here that Fraser was provided his first taste of sturgeon from the area.

> Here the Indians, who favoured us with the canoes thus far, left us and went home, and in consequence we were obliged to encamp. The Indians of this place promised to help us on tomorrow. They were extremely civil, insomuch as to force us to doubt their sincerity. They gave us plenty of sturgeon, oil, and roots, but which were not of the best quality or flavour.

It probably wasn't Fraser's first encounter with *Acipenser transmontanus* — he and his men had been fed mainly by the contributions of Native communities throughout his daunting voyages, and at that time the white sturgeon was plentiful throughout the Fraser River watershed. It is likely that these first few white men simply assumed that the sturgeon from the river that was later to bear Fraser's name was the same fish taken by Native people on the eastern slopes of the Rocky Mountains. But in those early days, there were those who suspected otherwise, noting that the sturgeon on the western side of the Rockies were greatly different from anything they had known. One of those was Daniel William Harmon, a trader with the Northwest Company at Stuart Lake, in the northern interior.

Harmon was a prolific diarist, and the picture that emerges from his journals stands in shocking contrast to later observations of the country and the people west of Prince George after disease, resource depletion and dispossession wasted the countryside. In Harmon's time, the country was an environment of almost unimaginable abundance — thousands of Native people lived in the vicinity of Stuart Lake, and the fisheries resources of the Nechako River watershed included salmon, sturgeon, whitefish, "carp" and other species. It was not unusual for Harmon's traders to put away 25,000 salmon for the winter. From Harmon's Stuart Lake journal of 1817:

> In the month of June, we took out of this lake 21 sturgeon, that were from eight to twelve feet in length. One of them measured twelve feet two inches from its extreme points, four feet eleven inches around the middle, and would weigh from five hundred and fifty to six hundred pounds. All the sturgeon we have caught, on this side of the mountain, are far superior in flavour to any I ever saw in any other part of the world.

It was not until 1836 that the scientific community explained these reports of giant fish in the waters west of the Rocky Mountains. In that year, the sturgeon across the mountains were confirmed as members of a separate and distinct species.

In those days, the discovery and identification of new species followed a convention nowadays maintained in the discovery of new stars, with all its charming hubris, and as a consequence the full scientific name for the white sturgeon is *Acipenser transmontanus Richardson*, after Sir John Richardson, the first white man to identify the white sturgeon as a wholly different species of fish, clearly of the order Acipenserformes, but unlike any other. He named it transmontanus, since it came from "across the mountains," and it makes its first appearance in the scientific literature on page 278 of Richardson's mammoth *Fauna Boreali-Americana; or The Zoology of the Northern Parts of British America, Part the Third, The Fish.*

Richardson is probably known best for his service as the surgeon and naturalist assigned to the expeditions in search of the fabled

Northwest Passage led by his friend, Sir John Franklin. Richardson served with the Franklin expeditions of 1819–22 and 1825–27, and travelled thousands of miles overland and by canoe throughout the Northwest Territories. When Franklin resumed his arctic explorations in later years, Richardson was busy with his duties as senior physician at the Royal Naval Hospital at Haslar, near Portsmouth, but when Franklin and his men failed to return from their 1845 expedition, Richardson, who was 60 at the time, volunteered to join in the 1849 search efforts, which proved futile. Apart from his career as surgeon and his fame as an explorer, Richardson's four-volume *Fauna Boreali-Americana* remains one of the most thorough natural histories in Canadian literature. Richardson appears to have completed most of his contributions to *Fauna Boreali-Americana* while he was posted as chief medical officer at Melville Hospital in Chatham, England. The work contains 140 fish specimens, sometimes described in obscure nomenclature long since fallen from use. Much of the book derives from Richardson's own collection and field notes. He gathered them during the Franklin expeditions while at Cumberland House, at Fort Enterprise and at the mouth of the Coppermine River. There are fish from Penetanguishene on Lake Huron, and from Great Bear Lake.

Richardson was also sent sketches and descriptions, and sometimes specimens, from gentlemen and fur-trade officers throughout Canada and the United States. John James Audubon sent him fish from the Newfoundland coast. A Dr. Scouler of the Dublin Institute sent him a "curious salmon from the coast of New Caledonia," as mainland British Columbia was known then, which appears to be a chum salmon in final spawning metamorphosis.

And one day "a cask full of specimens" arrived, "much damaged on the voyage," from a Dr. Gairdner. On the other side of the world, on the other side of the Rocky Mountains, at the mouth of the Columbia River, Simon Fraser's intended destination.

Gairdner reported:

The species attains eleven feet in length, and a weight of six hundred pounds; the small specimens sent home were chosen for their portability. It enters the Columbia early in March every year, and is caught as high up as Fort Colville, notwithstanding the numerous cataracts and rapids, which seem to be insuperable barriers to a fish so sluggish in its movements. It disappears about the month of September. It is termed by the Cheenooks katlook, and in the language of the Cascade Indians nakhun.

Was this the same gigantic animal that appears in Harmon's journals? Richardson raised the question, then left it alone, noting: "We have no means of ascertaining."

A quarter-century later, the popular literature begins taking notice of a creature in the Fraser River. In what is likely the white sturgeon's first published appearance in Canada, the New Westminster *Columbian* of July, 11, 1861, reports:

VERY LIKE A WHALE   The largest sturgeon we have ever seen was caught here last week. Its weight was 400 pounds, and length nine feet.

It was not until 1866, fully three decades after the publication of *Fauna Boreali-Americana*, that the Fraser River sturgeon was identified as *Acipenser transmontanus*, the same species of fish Dr. Gairdner sent Richardson from the Columbia River, in a cask, badly damaged on the voyage. This credit is due the Englishman John Keast Lord, veterinarian, author and vagabond. Lord dropped out of a veterinary practice in Tavistock, Devon, spent some time wandering around Arkansas, the Canadian prairies and the Ontario copper mines, then landed a job as the veterinarian and assistant naturalist with the 1858–1862 British North American Boundary Commission, cutting the 49th parallel through the bush from Point Roberts eastward. To Lord, Natives were almost always redskins and usually crafty or wily. In his otherwise valuable contribution to natural history, a work in two volumes entitled *The Naturalist in Vancouver Island and British Columbia*, published in 1866, Lord writes:

> During the time the Fraser and Columbia rivers are rising — and the rise is very rapid, about thirty feet above the winter level, owing to the melting snow — sturgeon are continually leaping. As you are quietly paddling along in a canoe, suddenly one of these monsters flings itself into the air many feet above the surface of the water, falling back again with a splash, as though a huge rock had been pitched in the river by some Titan hand.

Throughout this century, the human population has grown by the hundreds of thousands throughout the Fraser Valley. They commute in and out of Abbotsford and Chilliwack and Langley and New Westminster and Vancouver, from the suburbs of Sumas and South Surrey and Deroche and Maple Ridge. There are hundreds of thousands of gallons of sewage and industrial waste pumped into the Fraser River every day. In its last 100 miles, after pouring out of the canyon above Hope, the river has been channelled, diked, dredged and buried over. Still, every so often these 1,000-pound monsters turn up, living dinosaurs that emerged just this side of the Jurassic period 98 million years ago and stopped evolving about two million years ago. Every so often, they still emerge from the muddy depths of the Fraser River, where they have been spending their lives sucking up dead fish and anything else that rolls along the river bottom through an appendage that serves as a mouth but looks more like the severed stub of an elephant's trunk. They get trapped in somebody's net, or on somebody's hook, or crushed between the logs in a log boom, and the few witnesses to these events are briefly reminded of a long-forgotten beast that still exists below the bridges they commute across every day. A fish that looks like a cross between an antediluvian shark and a giant catfish, half blind, with five widely separated rows of pointed, bony shields called scutes in place of a skeleton. It is capable of surviving in water deep and muddy and bereft of oxygen where no other fish could survive. It can engage its body in a bizarre process that has excited the attention of neurologists studying phenomena related to comas in human beings — the sturgeon has the capacity to enter into a state of suspended animation so pronounced that it is not unlike death, willed upon itself, and from which it can emerge at will.

We know that white sturgeon have occurred only in a handful of rivers on North America's west coast, like the Sacramento, San Joaquin, Columbia and the Fraser. We do not know how old they can get. There are ways to determine the age of individual fish. There is the otolith, a tiny bone from the ear, and there is also a ray that sticks out of the sturgeon's pectoral fin, which looks like a human finger. In both instances, you count the growth rings, just like a tree. A 700-pounder caught at Dewdney Slough in 1977 was judged to be 132 years old.

They are known to gorge themselves on spawned-out salmon, lying in wells 30 metres deep at the bottom of the river in the Fraser Canyon, which at its most violently constricted is like the open palm of a human hand turned on edge, the width no greater than the thumb, the depth as great as the thumb and four fingers in line. And they lie in wait down there hoping for dead fish to tumble in on top of them. They'll eat just about anything. Stomach contents have turned up rocks, birds, and a cat, but more routinely, sturgeon eat crayfish, lampreys, sculpins and sticklebacks. They are said to lie in wait in deep trenches of their own construction in the muddy river bottom below Hope, trenches that collect the carcasses of spawned-out salmon and oolichan, and anything else that might roll along in the dark. Carl Leon remembered a farmer on Barnston Island who was walking along the riverbank when he heard a rustling in the undergrowth, and when he pulled the briars aside he found a giant sturgeon thrashing in the roots of a cottonwood tree, where it had emerged from the sand after burrowing into the river bottom from a trench it had dug out in the river somewhere. And there were people who insisted that the reason the old Mission Bridge collapsed was that its footings were undermined by sturgeon caves.

There were old Sto:lo sturgeon fishermen who said that people who fell from their canoes and whose bodies were never found became sturgeon, or lived among the sturgeon. The memory of these stories is fading, but what's sure is that the white sturgeon are somehow involved in the whereabouts of the souls of those who drown and whose bodies are never recovered from the river.

III

THE BARB OF THE SPEAR IMMEDIATELY DISCONNECTS FROM THE POLE

The occasional dead sturgeon might not be any cause for alarm, but in the days following September 13, 1993, when Rosenau took Annie Van den Berg's call from Derby Reach, more giant sturgeon started washing up dead on the banks of the river. On Thursday that week, Dennis McKamey from Northside Cedar in Mission called up to report a dead 12½-footer. It weighed more than 800 pounds and turned out to be more than 100 years old. The following Monday Rosenau got a call from Todd Chapman, a platoon sergeant with the Lower Fraser Aboriginal Fisheries Commission. An 11-footer had washed up dead at Katz Bay near the Chawathil reserve, just downstream from Hope. ¶ Already on extinction's cliff-edge, the prospect of the white sturgeon going over that last precipice loomed closer. At the bottom of the cliff, there was already the Strait of Georgia halibut, 100-pounders that gave their name to Halibut Bank, in the same way sturgeon had given their name to Sturgeon Bank, north of Sand Heads at the Fraser's mouth. Halibut were fished by handline in English Bay and Burrard Inlet in the 1880s, and now there were none left. Gone,

FACING PAGE: *Captain John of Soowahlie, who warned in 1894 of the "wholesale slaughter" of sturgeon in the Fraser River.* ROYAL BRITISH COLUMBIA MUSEUM (PN8918)

too, are the humpback whales of Georgia Strait, a distinct population that lasted until January of 1908, when the last pod was slaughtered with exploding harpoons off the mouth of the Fraser.

For all Marvin could tell, this creature, too, whose lineage began with Clothed-With-Power's daughter, and who was involved somehow when people were lost to the river, their bodies never recovered, was about to vanish. Something was happening down there at the bottom of the river. Rosenau didn't know what it was, how to stop it or where it would end. The telephone calls, reports of dead sturgeon washed up on the riverbank, kept coming in.

And before it was all over he would find himself gasping for air, fighting for his life and struggling against the violent rapids in the depths of the Fraser Canyon. He barely survived the ordeal, but there would be a death. A drowning in the river, and a body not recovered.

Around the time the sturgeon that had washed up at Derby Reach, Northside Cedar and Katz Bay were emerging from their eggs, the Sto:lo shaman-turned-preacher Captain John of Soowahlie, speaking on behalf of five Chilliwack chiefs, was telling B.C. Indian Superintendent A.W. Vowell: "We would like you as our chief to enter protest against the wholesale slaughter of sturgeon in the Fraser River . . . now that the white people are about to destroy what seems to us our last resort, we think the time has come for us to speak." That was April 26, 1894. The giants that were washing up on Fraser River sandbars had somehow survived the "wholesale slaughter" that wiped out their parents' generation, and now, after all these years, they were showing up dead and there was no telling why.

Two days after Chapman's call, another dead sturgeon was reported at Harbour Air in New Westminster, below the old B.C. Penitentiary, near the mouth of the Brunette River, at the site where Government House once was, more than a century earlier. In the 1860s, the colonial secretary, Sir Arthur Nonas Birch, used to look up from his desk at Government House and gaze out over the broad sweep of the Fraser to watch Sto:lo people fishing sturgeon. On May 7, 1864, he wrote his brother, John:

> I have got a very nice little wooden office and my room is charming now though I fear very cold in the winter. All the Indians now fishing and it is great fun to watch them spearing sturgeon which here run to the enormous size of 500 and 600 lbs. The Indians drift down with the stream perhaps 30 canoes abreast with their long poles with spear attached kept within a foot of the bottom of the river. When they feel a fish lying they raise the spear and thrust it at the fish seldom missing. The barb of the spear immediately disconnects from the pole but remains attached to a rope and you see sometimes two or three canoes being carried off at the same time downriver at any pace by these huge fish.

There was a slaughterhouse nearby, at the mouth of the Brunette River. Offal was routinely pitched into the water. The reach of the Fraser River outside Birch's window remained a thriving sturgeon-fishing ground through the 1880s, and in 1887, the British Columbia fisheries inspector had this to say about sturgeon:

> These fish still continue plentiful in the Fraser River. There are no regular sturgeon fisheries in this province yet, freight rates being too high to allow of a profitable trade in fresh sturgeon. The few that are now caught are taken mostly in salmon nets, thus giving the large breeding fish of from 200 to 600 pounds every chance of escape. I have had a number of enquiries with regards to the size, condition and quantity of sturgeon eggs at different seasons of the year, such enquiries being made with a view of engaging into the caviar trade. This industry, once opened, would soon become important, the more so as the fish are of excellent quality, and the flesh can be smoked or dried, when it will fetch fair prices if exported.

Fraser River.
Sturgeon.
13 ft 6 in. 905 lbs
head 188 lbs.

Caught by fisherman Jim Burgess near Douglas Island, at the mouth of the Coquitlam River, on Good Friday, 1912. This photograph, by W.T. Cooksley, was placed in the window of Monk's fish store on Front Street. At the time, the New Westminster Columbian *reported that the picture was "exciting considerable attention locally."* DELTA MUSEUM AND ARCHIVES

For decades, Sto:lo fishermen had traded portions of their sturgeon catch to the Hudson's Bay Company, which in turn marketed the isinglass from the sturgeon's swim bladder for use as a clarifying agent in the making of beer and jams and jellies, for waterproofing and as a pottery cement. Apart from that, the sturgeon catch went mainly to local markets. The total B.C. sturgeon catch (almost exclusively Fraser River) in 1887 amounted to 249,000 pounds. The 1888 B.C. fisheries inspector's report shows salmon landings at the New Westminster canneries, and counts of sea otter skins from the Bering Sea and walrus ivory from the Arctic Ocean. He says this about sturgeon:

> The demand for this fish in local markets seems to be increasing, large numbers being shipped to Victoria and Vancouver and to towns on Puget Sound and the interior. I have had numerous enquiries with a view to opening up a trade in the manufacture of caviar, but as yet no one has made it his regular business to catch them. The fish taken for market are usually caught with hook and line by natives and in salmon nets by local fishermen. The Fraser is the only river in this province where sturgeon are caught in any quantity. They appear to have no regular time for spawning, as they are caught full of ova a long distance upriver, and in the same condition during the months of May and June on the sand heads. It is estimated that only every tenth fish taken in the Fraser River is found to contain eggs.

The total B.C. sturgeon catch in 1888, almost exclusively from the Fraser River, was 215,000 pounds. All this was about to change.

East of the Rocky Mountains, the various species of sturgeon had been fished by European settlers from the days of the Virginia colonists in the 1620s. The eastern sturgeon were not small fish. Shortnose sturgeon are usually three feet in length, but lake sturgeon five feet in length and 100 pounds in weight were not uncommon and

Atlantic sturgeon up to ten feet in length had been reported throughout the maritime provinces and New England. For the most part, though, sturgeon were considered "Indian food," fit only for hogs, slaves and fertilizer, and as a consequence, Atlantic, lake and shortnose sturgeon survived in abundance well into the 1800s.

By the mid-1800s, however, overfishing caused a decline in the European sturgeon fisheries, and on that continent, particularly in Germany, new markets for caviar were opening up. On the eastern seaboard and in Ontario and Quebec, smoked sturgeon was becoming sought after in the wake of the public's growing taste for smoked halibut. Intensive fisheries were underway soon after North America's first successful caviar production began at Sandusky, Ohio, in 1855, and smoked sturgeon began to find a place in the market in 1860.

By 1885, more than five million pounds of lake sturgeon were taken out of Lake Erie. Ten years later, the catch was down to 200,000 pounds. At Lake of the Woods, sturgeon landings dropped 90 per cent over the same period. Through the 1890s, one fishery after another simply vanished. The Delaware River fishery collapsed, and the same pattern followed throughout the Great Lakes, New Jersey, Minnesota, the Carolinas and Pennsylvania. One by one, rivers were fished out, lakes were fished out, and by 1910, W.S. Tower of the University of Pennsylvania was moved to write: " . . . it seems scarcely comprehensible that a fish so widely distributed through the country, so abundant, and so little used less than three decades ago, has so rapidly disappeared that the end is already in sight."

After the eastern sturgeon populations were decimated, harvesters turned to the west. The west was opened with the railroads, and the Columbia River harboured the biggest sturgeon of them all. In 1888 a rail shipment of 180,000 pounds of frozen white sturgeon left Oregon for the eastern markets. Four years later, in 1892, 5.5 million pounds of white sturgeon from the Columbia River headed east. The Columbia fishery crashed. By the turn of the century,

Leif Wike of the Westminster Fish Company with a 624-pounder caught in 1949. WESTMINSTER FISH COMPANY

sturgeon fishermen in the Columbia were landing less than 100,000 pounds.

That left the Fraser River. By the early 1890s, two American firms had arrived in New Westminster from the Columbia River. They were Wallace and Company and Trescott and Company, "sturgeon freezers and exporters." Trescott boasted of its ability to put 20,000 hooks in the river between Mission and Steveston. Other companies joined in. There were warnings from some observers who were the conservationists of the day. There were people like "Lex," as a frequent contributor to the New Westminster *Columbian* newspaper was known to readers. In that newspaper's May 28, 1894, edition, he argued:

> When British Columbia invites capitalists, she wants them to come and stay, and not exhaust our resources, in a few years, then leave the country to hunt for another victim.

There was talk about stiff regulations and a firm closed season, and what little rules were imposed were based largely on regulations governing the eastern fisheries. Regulations did not sit well with the New Westminster board of trade, which argued against such interference in free enterprise. On the board's behalf, D. Robson wrote:

> However valuable the sturgeon fishery may seem from a theoretical point of view, they will always rate a very poor figure in the national assets if they are forever to remain in the river.

The sturgeon fishery was growing by leaps and bounds, and for the Sto:lo fishermen who depended so heavily on the sturgeon, the time had come, in the words of Captain John of Soowahlie, "to enter protest against the wholesale slaughter of sturgeon in the Fraser River." On March 12, 1894, Indian Superintendent A.W. Vowell, in Victoria, received a petition, signed by 158 Native people from several communities, from Tsawwassen to Nicomen. The petition asked that action be taken to curtail the fishery and to bring an end to the destructive American fishing methods the industry had introduced.

It greaves [sic] us to think that the white people are allowed their means which will soon kill sturgeon life in the Fraser River.

The petition concluded in the manner common to such entreaties:

Trusting you will give this matter your earliest consideration,
We have the honour to be, Sir,
Your obedient servants
    Cassimere, Indian Chief, Langley, and 15 others
    Tzats-ell-ton, Nicomen Slough, and 25 others
    Augustine, Matsqui, and 15 others
    Phiddell, Whonnock, and 9 others
    Swan-i-set, Katsie, and 26 others
    Johnny Punch, Coquitlam, and 8 others
    Johnny Quie-qui-aluck, Musqueam, and 32 others
    Harry, Chewasson, and 18 others.

The petition produced a flurry of letters between the various centres of bureaucracy. Vowell forwarded the letter to Hayter Reed, the deputy superintendent-general of Indian Affairs in Ottawa. He also sent copies to the local fisheries department officials and Fraser Valley Indian agent Frank Devlin. Devlin sat at his typewriter at the old Indian agent's office on Agnes Street in New Westminster and wrote back to Vowell setting out what he knew about the sturgeon fishery, which, in his view, amounted to "wholesale destruction" and threatened to eliminate "all the sturgeon in the Fraser River."

Two weeks after the Fraser Valley Natives sent in their petition, Methodist missionary C.M. Tate, Moral Governor of the Coqualeetza industrial school in Chilliwack (where the work of converting Sto:lo people to the Methodist faith was well underway), wrote to Vowell urging him to do something about the excesses of the sturgeon fishery. He enclosed an article from the Victoria *Times*:

> Something should be done to protect the sturgeon of the Fraser River. The Columbia has been cleaned of them long ago, and if the present unrestricted and wholesale slaughter continues another season the Fraser River will contain but few . . . The river is lined with fishermen at present, and the sturgeon are ensnared in every form that the device of man can accomplish.

In Ottawa, Reed passed on Vowell's letter and the Native petition to William Smith, deputy minister of marine and fisheries. A week later, Reed sent Smith a copy of Devlin's letter. A month after that, on May 7, Devlin received a letter. This time, it was from four Chilliwack chiefs. The four chiefs — Captain George Louis (Yakweakwioose), Joe X (Kwakwawapilt), Mottist X (Squay) and Peter X (Squiala) – pointed out that they were Catholics, and for that reason they were disinclined to join the majority of the Natives in the vicinity who wanted to deal directly with the white sturgeon fishermen, "by force."

> A good many whitemen are yet fishing now near Harrison River, openly stealing our fish, our only food. They want to see us starving, we cannot bear it. Our Chief and all our Indians want to go to-morrow and take by force the hooks, which these whitemen are using and send them away. We four other Catholic Chilliwack Chiefs think it better to wait a little before taking such a step and so we decided together to write to you.

Devlin was given until the following Monday. If their decision to give the government a chance proved fruitless, the chiefs said they intended to take matters into their own hands and "stop those fisher-

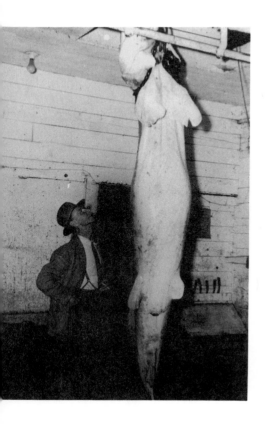

Frank Horley with a sturgeon caught in the Chilliwack area, 1950s.
CHILLIWACK MUSEUM AND
HISTORICAL SOCIETY (P7529)

men." A day after the Catholic chiefs wrote Devlin, Devlin wrote to Vowell in Victoria, pointing out that nothing had been done about the Natives' complaints about the Fraser River sturgeon fishery. He noted that "several members of the Board of Trade" were interested in investing in the sturgeon fishery, which would account for their influence with fisheries officials. Still, Devlin said he had written the Chilliwack chiefs and advised them to "leave the matter entirely in the hands of the government" and to leave the white fishermen alone. Devlin reiterated his observations about the fishery. He had earlier described the fishing methods to Vowell: Set-lines were placed on the river bottom, bank to bank, with baited hooks set 12 inches apart. Hauled up in the morning, all hooked sturgeon less than four feet in length were thrown back, dead and injured — many with two or three hooks in them. The Indians weren't likely to sit back much longer.

> Unless some action is taken by the Fishery Department to prevent the
> use of the apparatus now used by those fishermen, I am not sure I will
> be able to restrain the Indians. The mode of fishing at present carried
> on by those fishermen is most destructive, and if permitted to continue,
> will certainly deplete the River of sturgeon. It is a most rascally trap.

The fisheries department responded to all these interdepartmental memoranda by promising steps to ensure that sturgeon would be caught only by gillnets and handlines, but fisheries inspector John McNab made it plain what he thought of all the fuss. Sturgeon were caught by Fraser River fishermen, McNab wrote on May 8 to the minister in Ottawa. "As they receive good prices, the industry has been of great benefit to them," he said. This is the same McNab who looked the other way that same year when the Fraser River salmon canneries were engaged in mass salmon poaching. When Marshall English had 40 of his salmon licences cancelled for repeated violations of fisheries regulations, he fished his entire fleet that season anyway. Henry Bell-

Irving was licensed for 33 boats to supply his Steveston canneries, but McNab looked the other way when Bell-Irving fished 74 boats. When the fisheries department hired an investigator to work under McNab and look into various alleged violations, McNab tipped off the canneries. When the investigator refused to keep quiet about his findings, McNab fired him. As for all this business about juvenile sturgeon being hauled up dead after spending the night fighting hooks embedded in them, McNab wrote: "As they are a hardy fish, I do not think they are materially injured."

In Ottawa, Hayter Reed was unimpressed. In a letter to William Smith, McNab's boss, Reed pointed to the letters from Devlin and the Chilliwack chiefs. He wrote:

> . . . the matter is more serious than it seemed to the Inspector of Fisheries to be, and it is hoped that you will be able to take some step to put a stop to what is complained of.

The federal government had no sturgeon-fishing regulations until late in 1894, and fisheries officials insisted that there would not be a repeat of the American experience. According to one 1894 fisheries department circular:

> The Department feels justified in preventing a repetition of the wholesale and reckless destruction by foreign capitalists of an industry which is year by year becoming more valuable to our people.

"Brawl lines," as they were known, were outlawed. But the fishery expanded anyway.

By the end of 1894, the total sturgeon catch on the Fraser River amounted to 452,000 pounds, worth more than $20,000. There was even a market for their cartilage: 809 pounds of sturgeon "bones," worth $407, were sold.

As the years passed, the catch increased.

In 1897, a total of 1,137,696 pounds of sturgeon was taken out of the Fraser River. That is roughly the weight of 7,000 people, which is roughly the population of New Westminster at the time. The landed value of sturgeon that year: $56,884. The following year, a northeast wind blew through the city of New Westminster, pushing a wall of flames before it. The docks were soon ablaze, along with the stern-wheelers tied to them. The farmer's market was in flames. So was the Canadian Pacific Navigation warehouse, the public library, Holy Trinity Cathedral and the Opera House. Even the firehall was gutted. There was little left of the city. But the sturgeon fishery continued.

In 1898, the catch fell to 750,000 pounds.

In 1899, the catch had fallen to 278,000 pounds. In his report for that year, fisheries inspector McNab wrote:

It is too early to say whether this falling off is occasioned by the deple-tion of the river or merely one of those fluctuations to which all fishing industries are liable.

But the catch continued to fall. In 1900, only 105,000 pounds of sturgeon were brought in — one tenth the amount harvested in 1897.

As the returns fell, the number of sturgeon licences McNab issued also declined: 164 in 1898, 88 in 1899, 23 in 1900, 22 in 1901, and 5 in 1902. That year, only 33,500 pounds were harvested. McNab wrote:

It would not appear that we are ever likely again to see this fishery of any commercial importance. The cold storage companies take all that they can get, but the supply, especially of the larger fish, is very limited.

By 1905, the Sto:lo sturgeon fisheries were being curtailed by force. As the Chilliwack *Progress* noted, on April 26, 1905:

The commercial sturgeon catch on the Fraser, measured in thousands of pounds. The scale on the left applies to catches up to 1920; the larger scale on the right measures post-1920 catches. BASED ON SEMAKULA AND LARKIN

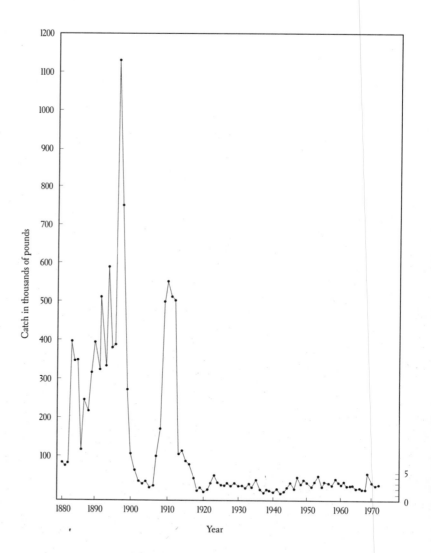

The Fisheries department sent a detective up to Sumas Lake and seized all the nets belonging to the Indians who were fishing for sturgeon in that lake . . . from the standpoint of the side of the Indians it is nothing short of a calamity, as at this season of the year their only livelihood has been taken away, and they are consequently in a state of destitution.

Sumas Lake, where the detective was sent to seize sturgeon nets from Sto:lo fishermen, was a 30,000-acre shallow lake, a prime sturgeon fishing area, just west of present-day Chilliwack. In the last century, the sky was darkened by clouds of waterfowl, and the lake was teeming with "roundfish" and sturgeon. There were Sto:lo villages on the hills surrounding the lake and its adjoining prairies. It was described in 1866, in John Keast Lord's *The Naturalist in Vancouver Island and British Columbia*:

The crafty redskins had stages erected, or rather fashioned to stout poles driven like piles into the mud at the bottom of the lake. To these platforms over the water they will retire, on the first appearance of mosquitos.

. . . These stages each with a family of Indians living on them, have a most picturesque appearance. The little fleet of canoes are moored to the poles and the platforms reached by a ladder made of twisted cedar bark. Often I have slept on these stages among the savages, to avoid being devoured. If you are restless and roll about in your sleep, you stand a very good chance of finding yourself soused in the lake.

In those days, Sumas Lake drained into the Fraser River by way of a short watercourse, where the Sumas people maintained a sturgeon weir. The weir was reported to be about 100 yards wide and 20 to 25 feet deep. Its braces and latticework allowed smaller fish to pass. In the early mornings, sturgeon would be found in the clear water, resting against the weir. Fishermen would walk out along a boardwalk constructed the length of the weir, and the sturgeon were harvested by harpoon, and sometimes by rope in a kind of lasso.

In 1920, the draining of Sumas Lake was begun. There were 30,000 acres of valuable farmland under shallow water to be reclaimed. The federal government "owned" it, and turned it over to the provincial government, which sold the lake bottom to farmers. On July 4, 1923, after three years of construction and earthworks, the pumps were turned on. In the spring of 1924, ploughing and seeding began. By the autumn of that year, the final 10,000 acres were drained. Stories persist in the valley about farmers ploughing up live sturgeon in the marshy sections of their fields as late as the 1930s.

Less than 30 years after sturgeon entered the mainstream of North American industrial fisheries, they were extirpated from much of their traditional range and pushed to the brink of extinction. The only sturgeon to escape a frontal assault was the mysterious and rare green sturgeon, the final species to reveal itself to western science. Known on both sides of the North Pacific, the green sturgeon, which has been known to reach lengths of seven feet, has shown up at the mouth of the Fraser and the Skeena, off Kyuquot on Vancouver Island's northwest coast, off Victoria and off the coast of Korea, China, Japan and Kamchatka. The first recorded Canadian specimen was turned in to the British Columbia Provincial Museum in 1908.

IV

SADDLE ROCK

The same day Marvin Rosenau was alerted to the eight-foot dead sturgeon at Harbour Air's docks below the old B.C. Penitentiary, at the site of the old Government House where Sir Arthur Birch watched sturgeon fishing from his window in the 1860s, another call came in. A ten-footer was discovered at the mouth of the Vedder River. It had been hauled across the Fraser to Nicomen Slough. A week later, Catherwood Towing called in from Mission with another 12½-footer. Two days later, Port Hammond Cedar Products reported one the same size at their docks. The reports kept coming, from the Peters Reserve near Herrling Island, a few minutes west of Hope on the 401, to the Roberts Bank coal port causeway, just above the Tsawwassen ferry terminal. ¶ In little more than a month, Marvin's notes showed 14 "really-solid-for-sures" and another half-dozen to a dozen "not-so-for-sures." It was hard to say what it all meant. Nobody knew how many sturgeon remained in the Fraser River. It was conceivable that a few hundred of the old giants were still there, but it was just as plausible that only a few dozen remained. All these fish were showing up dead, but there was no way of knowing how many deaths were going unreported.

Rosenau sent sturgeon carcasses to the laboratories for various tests. He put out the word to the river's Sto:lo fishing families and to the small and peculiar fraternity of hook-and-line sturgeon fishermen from places like Vedder Crossing and Floods, and to that handful of characters in salmon gillnetters who cling stubbornly to the deadhead-strewn reaches of the river upstream of New Westminster. He asked everyone to be on the lookout for "sick" sturgeon. Or at least try to bring in a big, live one, since it's almost impossible to conduct a proper disease analysis on an already rotting and bug-ridden fish.

When the laboratory tests came back, Rosenau started to get really worried, but not because of what the tests produced. It was because they produced nothing. They tested for polychlorinated biphenyls, 19 metals, 23 organochlorines, 17 dioxins and furans, and nothing turned up — at least nothing at a level so high as to make the fish unsafe for human consumption, let alone high enough to kill a fish. Tzeachten Indian band chief Kenny Malloway caught a live six-footer in his gill-net in the Fraser Canyon and brought it in. Ministry staff watched it closely in its pen at the Fraser Valley trout hatchery in Sumas. Bacteriologists and pathologists and hematologists studied every inch of the beast and turned up no evidence of anything that might explain what was killing so many sturgeon.

And there were the rumours. A helicopter pilot called in with a story that suggested hundreds of dead sturgeon floating downstream below Mission Bridge, but they turned out to be nothing more than dead, spawned-out pink salmon. One rumour had it that federal fisheries officials underestimated salmon-run sizes and ordered salmon hatchery staff to set off explosive charges at the mouths of hatcheries to prevent overspawning of hatchery-bound salmon, killing sturgeon in the process. And there were theories. One report fingered the fallout from an RCMP burn of confiscated marijuana in a beehive burner near Boston Bar. Another story pointed to a clandestine dump of toxins into the Upper Fraser in the days before the first dead giants started washing up.

Some anglers reported sluggish, decrepit-looking sturgeon too sick to put up a fight after they'd been hooked. Others said the fishing had never been so good, and the sturgeon were fighting as fiercely as ever.

Rosenau was left with a mystery on his hands and few leads. After the lab tests came back, it was hard to say even where he should start looking. "I didn't know if these were the only fish that would show up dead, or whether there would be hundreds, or what, and then having no way to do anything about it."

All Rosenau could say was that an "event" had occurred in the depths of the river, and whatever it was, it was powerful enough to kill 1,000-pound fish without leaving a trace. And these were not easy fish to kill. Over the years, there were stories along the river about sturgeon left for dead on the riverbank and kicked back into the river days later, only to swim away.

An event had occurred down there. Beyond that, Rosenau couldn't say much. By late September 1993, Rosenau was left with little to go on and a lot of worries about justifying the expense of elaborate laboratory studies to senior ministry staff. The dead sturgeon reports were piling up and there wasn't much evidence to review except dates, descriptions and points on a map. Studies in radio-tagging in the mid-1980s suggested that sturgeon — at least the big ones — stake out a stretch of river bottom and stay there, probably for decades. They might move a mile or two, but that's about it. Studies in California suggested that white sturgeon spawn in rocky, boulder-strewn waters, and it appears likely that juvenile Fraser River sturgeon are swept downstream to the Fraser estuary where they remain until they reach sexual maturity at 20 years old or so, when they return upriver to spawn, and eventually find a slough they like enough to stay.

Rosenau looked at the points on the map where the dead sturgeon

The first of the 1993 mortalities.
This was the creature that washed up
on the riverbank at Derby Reach,
near Annie Van den Berg's house.
MARVIN ROSENAU

had washed up, and he decided they'd probably been swept downstream from the place where the "event" had occurred. Everything pointed in the direction of the Fraser Canyon.

At 9 a.m. on the morning of Tuesday, September 28, 1993, Marvin headed out on a Lower Fraser Aboriginal Fisheries Commission patrol boat with LFAFC officers Wayne Kelly and James Adams, bound for the canyon. Rosenau wasn't quite sure what he was expecting to find. It was a beautiful morning.

All he remembers about what happened is that about two hours after setting out from Bristol Island, Kelly was at the helm of the patrol boat, and as they neared Saddle Rock, about four miles above Yale, in the violent cataract of the canyon, Kelly lost control. The vessel was drawn backward into the curl of a standing wave. It flipped.

Rosenau's memory contains jumbled pieces. He was washed up on the west bank of the river more than half a mile downstream. He rested for a few minutes on the rocks. Then he climbed the canyon wall to the highway where he attempted to flag down passing motorists. There were German tourists who didn't know what he was talking about, then he remembers a second vehicle, and finally a department of highways road crew worker who managed to get the word out.

An hour or so later, a chopper from Fraser Valley Helicopters hoisted Kelly out of a crevice on the east wall of the canyon, by cable and sling. James Adams was lost, presumed drowned after extensive search efforts failed to recover his body. James was 23 years old, a member of the Katzie Indian band, that small Sto:lo community who count a sturgeon among their myth-time ancestors. James was a husband and a father of two small children. His nickname was "Stick" because he was so skinny. RCMP Staff Sgt. Ed Hill said the search for James Adams was probably one of the most intensive of its kind in B.C. history. Hope Search and Rescue, LFAFC and federal fisheries' patrol boats, dozens of Sto:lo fishermen, RCMP and private helicopters, an RCMP dive team, psychics, members of the Lummi, Swinomish and Skagit tribal authorities in Washington state, recruits from the First Nations Tribal Police Institute, the Coast Guard hovercraft, sportsfishermen and commercial fishermen scoured the river from Saddle Rock to Steveston. They turned up nothing.

Rosenau didn't turn up anything in his efforts, either. After James was lost, the reports of dead sturgeon dropped off. Three or four came in, but it was hard to say how long they'd been dead. And whatever was happening down at the bottom of the river, the evidence was no longer pointing to the canyon. One report came in from Pitt Lake. The last find came from Harrison Lake. And then it was all over.

In the end, there was no neat scientific conclusion, nothing to establish confidence in any remedy and no tidy cause-and-effect. Rosenau lost his field notes in the canyon that day, but they weren't that important anymore. He could reconstruct what he needed from memory and his colleagues' notes, but by then it didn't really matter.

In the year that had passed since Stick died, nothing revealed itself. Rosenau was beginning to suspect a remote possibility of some sort of undocumented plankton bloom that contaminates the fresh water clams sturgeon sometimes root from the river bottom. He wouldn't lay claim to so much as a gut feeling about what it all meant. Maybe low river levels and higher-than-usual water temperatures had something to do with it, or some natural phenomenon that may have been aggravated by global warming, but obscure enough to reduce scientific inquiry to speculation. Maybe some kind of sickness. Marvin would admit to a personal opinion that whatever happened in the final weeks of summer in 1993, there should be no harvest of sturgeon permitted anymore. Between 1985 and 1991, the number of sturgeon anglers had tripled, but the number of fish per angler was dropping. While the total number of sturgeon caught was on the rise, the number of juvenile sturgeon showing up was dropping. His own government's one-fish-a-year rule, above Mission Bridge, was probably too much. Below

October 4, 1993: Mark Green, a technician with the Fraser Valley Trout Hatchery, stands by a sturgeon found at the Tsawwassen coal port causeway.
MARVIN ROSENAU

Mission Bridge, where the federal government regulates the fishery, the one-fish-a-day rule was definitely unjustifiable. Nobody seemed to know how many sturgeon were showing up in the commercial salmon fishery in the river. At least nobody was prepared to guess.

The Committee on the Status of Endangered Wildlife in Canada classifies the white sturgeon as a "vulnerable" species, retreating from its ancient Fraser Basin habitats, and now exceedingly rare everywhere above the Fraser Canyon. Below the canyon, habitat loss and the various fisheries posed threats to what was left. The B.C. Conservation Data Centre rates the white sturgeon as "rare or uncommon — susceptible to large-scale disturbances." Whatever happened in 1993, it could easily be defined as a "large-scale disturbance." It was only by the most radical measures employed over several decades that fisheries managers had stabilized white sturgeon populations in the Columbia River. A mandatory live-release of all Fraser River sturgeon caught in every fishery — sports, commercial and tribal — was the only answer, Rosenau concluded. Shut the whole thing down. There was just no way to justify killing creatures like this anymore.

V

THESE PEOPLE,
AND SOME OTHERS,
WHO FELL FROM THE SKY

The sun has fallen to a point in the sky no higher than Mount Calamity now, and a loud splash echoes across the river. Probably nothing. Maybe a seal. They are known in the river this far from saltwater and they surprise people unfamiliar with the river, out in their boats. Seals are known to swim far up Harrison Lake, almost 100 miles from saltwater, and they swim up the mainstem of the river to the mouth of the Fraser Canyon, after oolichan and salmon, as though the valley were still merely an arm of the sea, a long narrow inlet with its head around Yale, more than 100 miles from the river-mouth. Hair seals. Commonly called harbour seals. They have been here in the river a long time. ¶ But not so long. It was only 18,000 years ago that the Cordilleran ice sheet was still pushing its way through all the valleys west of the Rocky Mountains, and north of the Cascades, to a depth exceeding 6,000 feet above what is now the Rosedale Bridge, suspended above the river upstream from where we are anchored. At the close of this ice age, another one began. The land was inundated again, and a glacier exceeding 700 feet in depth

FACING PAGE: *The Sto:lo fishermen (left to right) Alfred Cline, Joe Louie and Ed Louie, with their catch from the Fraser River at Dewdney Slough, date unknown.* CHILLIWACK MUSEUM AND HISTORICAL SOCIETY (P656)

Terry Glavin 55

covered the Fraser Valley. The valley was still an inlet of the sea that pushed into the mountains around Yale about 10,000 years ago, when the sisters of Cheam Peak wept as they looked down on the lifeless expanse of water and ice.

As the glaciers retreated, the salmon advanced into the expanses of cold and shallow water and gravel and pebble fields, and the seals advanced after the salmon, and then the trees took root in the rotting carcasses of spawned-out salmon. In the terraces above Yale, 9,000-year-old hearth sites mark the places where people roasted wild cherry, which become ripe at the time the sockeye ascend the river.

It was during this time of uncertainty and instability, at a place just a short stretch downstream from the place we are anchored, beyond Mount Calamity, that three men in a canoe rounded a point at the mouth of the Harrison River. They found three children playing in the water.

At the turn of the century, Casimir, the chief of the Scowlitz band, recounted this event to Charles Hill-Tout, a pioneer in the fields of archeology and anthropology in British Columbia. Hill-Tout was a schoolteacher who left his theological training in England after reading Huxley and Darwin and ended up a settler and justice of the peace in Abbotsford. Hill-Tout attended seances in Vancouver, where he founded Buckland College on Burrard Street, and spent several years learning Native languages and recording the origins of the people of this part of the world, from people like Casimir.

In the events that follow their encounter with the children in the water, the men in the canoe learn that there is something unusual about the people from the children's village. Every morning, the children of the village go down to the river to bathe, but when they return, one of them is always missing. And every morning, someone presents the three men with a fresh sturgeon. The men are told to be respectful of what they do not eat. To put the bones aside. The bones are returned to the river.

Every morning, a child went missing. Every morning, a missing child returned.

It was from these people that the Scowlitz descended, Casimir explained. These people, and some others, who fell from the sky. Hill-Tout was thankful to Casimir. He wrote this of him:

> The old people used to consider themselves under the care and guardianship of the spirit of the sturgeon, and his father had a sturgeon crest or sakwaiam. He did not care to talk about the subject much, as these topics are discountenanced by the priests; but although he is the leader of the daily services in the church, he has still much of the love of the Indian for the "old days" in him yet. . .

Mount Cheam, behind us, has turned ochre. It was from Mount Cheam that the Sto:lo people around here got their salt, for cooking sturgeon. Old Robert Joe, from Chilliwack, told anthropologist Wilson Duff about it in 1950. Duff's field notes record this:

> Cooking pots made of cedar or yellow cedar.
> Treated to take odor out of wood. Made into
> square buckets, up to 2' square. Sown with
> cedar bark and sealed with m a t
> [a glue obtained from a sturgeon's spine].
> Bottom same. Pot set on ground.
> Rocks 6" diam. certain kinds (some rocks
> will loudly explode or crumble when put in water)
> Dipped/washed in bucket of water to take sand
> and ashes off, then into boiler.
> 3 or 4 rocks make it boil. 2 batches
> will do anything.
> Got salt from Cheam Peak, It was

not exactly white, kind of brown, powdered,
and used sparingly.

The tip of the middle rod is bouncing.

"There's a bite on it," Nick says. His left arm shoots forward and grabs the rod's haft. Marvin throws back the canopy and it crashes over the windshield and we jump to our feet. Nick gives the rod a swift tug.

Nothing.

"I think it was a sturgeon," Nick says. "Maybe he was fussy about it, but it was a bite. Maybe he was leery about it. But it was definitely a bite."

I remind myself that this may take all night. And it may never happen. Robert Joe said some people are unlucky. He said:

Some of these would punish
themselves. Take cedar boughs (sharp
little scales on them), a bunch all gathered
up. Or used young spruce boughs. The
man that's unlucky goes down the river,
takes a good bath, rubs himself with these
all over, even down side of face.

We watch the rod tips for movement. Hook-and-line fishing is like that, but in the last century, this reach of the river was fished in a different way. One way was the sturgeon spear. Robert Joe said:

Paddle easy downstream — 2 bow men.
No noise. No talking. Use signs to bow
man. Signal him by jerking canoe a little.

You use a feather from the wing of an eagle, or a long piece of cedar bark, to feel your way along the bottom. That way, there's no noise from the end of the spear. The sturgeon doesn't know you're coming.

You use the same things with the xi'xamal. The xi'xamal is a bag net fixed to a long pole with a crutch at the bottom end. From where we are anchored, all the way down to the old Lakaway village near Chilliwack, you can use the xi'xamal. Downstream of Sumas Mountain, it wasn't any good. Here, the bottom is sandy. There are no snags.

And there was another kind of xi'xamal. It was bigger and required two poles and two canoes, the net suspended between them.

Poles. 24' long. Don't fish deeper than
that. Can feel fish in, pull poles up
and net closes. Always go downstream —
fish always face upstream.

Upriver a few miles, there was once a great sturgeon-fishing place. Maria Slough.

People went from here, Pilaltq, Nicomen,
etc. to fish at Maria Slough. Sometimes
15–20 canoes there. No one tribe
owned it. Main reason for going there
was get together, visit, picnic. Spring
and summer best.

All of a sudden the boat is rocking violently.

Jesus. What a hit, Nick says.

Nick has grabbed the port-side fishing rod, which is bending dangerously with the weight of something, and Marvin throws back the canopy again. It crashes on the bow, and we are all three on our feet.

My God, Nick says, laughing, and then he is not laughing. My God.

VI

THE EYES ARE LOOKING AT US

The line is tight and whatever it is on the end of it, it appears to be running downriver with the bait and the hook and the line, and Marvin is climbing over the windshield to free the bow line from the bright red scotchman float that holds the anchor line from the river bottom. ¶ Here, Nick says. Quick. And he is passing me the fishing rod. ¶ Or he is trying to pass me the fishing rod, which has become an inverted J. It is Marvin's rod. It is the small black rod with the $18.50 suggested retail price sticker still on it. The rod Marvin's dad bought at the Army and Navy in Vancouver in 1971 when Marvin was 15, the year after Marvin caught his first sturgeon down at the dock at Fraser Mills. The rod with all its old guides gone and new tungsten guides taped on in their place. The one Nick tied the big lamprey to. On a barbless hook. ¶ The bend in the rod is straightening itself and the angle of the line, shimmering in the glaring sunlight, is quickly declining until it appears almost parallel to the river. There is a sudden explosion of light and spray downstream. A sturgeon breaches from the surface and leaps into the light of day. It is as big as I am.

Nick is shouting. Did you see that? It's a big one. Did you see that?

Go ahead, Marvin shouts. Nick is passing me the rod. Seconds pass. The boat is free of its anchor line and we are drifting downstream.

Here you go, Nick says. He is straining with the tension on the rod. He is passing it to me. I take the rod in my left hand, about two feet up from the butt. I am left-handed. What do I do with my right hand?

I can jig for rockfish and lingcod and I can cast for salmon and I can stand in my waders in the wintertime and watch my float if I am fishing with people who know what they are doing, and in my best moments, I have been a flyfisherman. But I have no idea how to cope with something like this. I grab the butt of the rod with my right hand and jab my thumb onto the reel and resolve to do whatever Nick or Marvin tell me to do.

Maintain tension, Nick says. If she gives you a chance, reel in some line, but keep the line tight. Let her run if she has to, then reel it in some more when she tires.

The boat is following the fish. We are slowly spinning downriver. The boat sweeps in a circle under the fishing line. The 50-horsepower Johnson outboard passes underneath, and I remind myself to keep it clear. Don't let it tangle in the propeller. Nick ducks. I pass it over the bow as best I can. Marvin ducks. I raise the rod as high as I can. I reel in some line, lowering the rod at the same time. It is no use. We are whirling downstream and the rod is an inverted U, and it's everything I can do to keep my balance. Nick is watching his landmarks carefully. Somewhere around here there is a gravel reef jutting upriver. There is a submerged island up ahead. Which channel should we take? The boat is running closer and closer to the north bank, to a riprap dike of boulders and overhanging alder. Marvin has the oar over the side. I am not at all sure what he is doing. My muscles are straining. I hear the sound of the outboard, and Nick is trying to describe to Marvin what to watch for, what to avoid under the surface of the water. Then there is no sound from the outboard. There is a low island now, and I think we are running between it and the north bank. I raise the rod as high as I can, lowering it as I reel in the line, and I am aching. This goes on and on until the animal is directly below us. I am trying to pull it closer to the surface, and I am making some headway, but it is only because the animal is resting, and it allows itself to be brought closer and closer to the starboard side.

There is the bullet-shaped head.

There is the tail fin, cutting through the surface of the water.

There is the ridge of barbs down its back.

There is its silver-grey body.

There are its barbed scutes, enclosed in white diamonds like diamonds from a deck of cards, running in lines down its sides.

It is coming closer and closer and closer. It is translucent, like a ghost, and as the creature submarines past the boat I can see into its bright yellow eyes, and they are almost fluorescent. They are moving. The eyes are looking at us, to see what we are.

And then it is running away again, and I am blinded by the sun. The boat is rolling and I am losing my balance.

I let the reel spin under my thumb until I can hold the fish steady again, and begin reeling in line, pulling the animal closer, sitting on the edge of the back of a seat, propping the butt behind my knee, holding on as long and hard as I can until the beast is pulling too hard. It is running too fast.

And then it begins again. Pull hard, reel in. Pull hard, reel in. We are in a channel now, downstream of the boulders, and we are in shallows. The fish is tiring. Maybe just resting. I don't know how long this has been going on.

Then there is blinding sunlight again, and then the dark green of alder and cottonwood, and the shade of a mountain somewhere, pain in my arms and my back, glimpses of thick riverbank cottonwood, more blinding sunlight, and Nick's voice telling me, you're doing fine. I'm doing fine.

Marvin has fired up the engine again. The sturgeon is tiring. We are drifting closer to the bank, into the shallows. Marvin cuts the engine and pulls up the propeller. I am reeling in hard, and the sturgeon is alongside. Nick jumps out into knee-deep water. Marvin jumps out and steadies the boat. And then the sturgeon is beached, out of the current, and we pull the fish into a shallow pool at the edge of the river, on the rocky beach of what appears to be the mouth of a long-dormant and empty side channel. I have jumped out of the boat, and I am standing in the water, and Nick has taken the rod. The sturgeon is better than five feet in length, not quite six. I hear Nick's voice again. You did good, he says.

The lamprey, tied to the barbless hook, falls from the sturgeon's contracted mouth as though it hadn't even set. The sturgeon's tail is swaying in the shallow water. It is a beautiful creature. Its eyes are beautiful. I stumble up the beach, exhausted.

I try to get my bearings, but my orientation is completely gone. The sun has fallen behind a mountain. At least I imagine it has, because it is cool and dark.

VII

NOW YOU HAVE KILLED
THE GOD; YOU HAVE
WHAT YOU WANTED

There is a heavy growth of Douglas fir rising up a hillside, and what might be the mouth of a slow-moving creek, but there is no sound, only the slight tremor of leaves from the scrub willow over the beach. The river has fallen silent, nothing looks familiar to me, and I don't know where I am anymore. ¶ The creature's irridescent eyes are moving in its armour-plated head. The eyes survey what little they can, but the white sturgeon is a notoriously myopic creature. It senses food by smell, if that is how to describe the sensory information it deduces from the four finger-like barbels that protrude between its snout and its trunk-like mouth. So there is perhaps only bright sunlight, and strange images taking shape above the boot-deep pool at the river's edge where it lies now, its tail fin swaying in the shallow water. And maybe voices. ¶ I look around me. The shadows in the trees above the riverbank tell me where north is. There are poplars on an island in the river. There are the blue-peaked mountains in the east. There is the sturgeon in its shallow pool. And I realize that this is the first time in my life that I have actually seen the Fraser River white sturgeon in the wild.

There is Mount Cheam. This is the Agassiz side, then, just across Cemetery Hill from the place where the Chehalis reserve schoolteacher J.W. Burns listened to stories and turned them into an essay about the Sasquatch, in 1929, for *Maclean's* magazine, which began the slow extinction of an old idea and the gradual emergence of a creature that shares a fanciful taxonomy with ghosts, those terrifying swamp animals from the Burnaby flats, the creatures from the tunnels under the streets of New Westminster, the giant water monster that was rumoured to live in the depths of the river and the imagined sturgeon in Hartog's bestiary that swims through the still-glowing beams of sunken locomotives.

At the sprung doors of the fireboxes, still warm, the sturgeon hover. They nibble at the live glowing coals — a delicacy wrung from them in turn by fishermen, for the market; where gourmets buy the bright red eggs of the locomotives in jars, to spread on toast.

There are giant serpents people see in Lake Aylmer and Lake Pohenegamook and Lake Saint François in Quebec. There is the beast in New York's Lake Champlain and the monster of Okanagan Lake. And the giant sturgeon remains the only rational explanation for any of them, perhaps the last inhabitant of the dark corridor between what is real and what is imagined, between zoology and cryptozoology.

We see this fish, we see monsters.

At Loch Ness in Scotland, where sturgeon once swam in thick schools, 19th-century reports of a huge fish in the lake evolved into rumours of a monster. A 1993 survey of the ecological productivity of Loch Ness concluded that the lake has been so degraded that it can now support a population of perhaps ten large sturgeon, but there are no sturgeon left there anyway.

Between what we can understand and what we imagine, there is the giant white sturgeon.

The fish lies quietly, beautiful and alone in its shallow pool. There is nothing to explain it. There is only Carl Leon, turning in his chair in his darkened office at the foot of Bonson Road in 1981, the man who never lived to see inside Thunderbird Hole. He places the bag of charred bones into a drawer, and tries to explain that actually the creature is the daughter of Clothed-With-Power, who became a sturgeon.

In Margaret Atwood's "Oratorio for Sasquatch, Man and Two Androids, " Android 1 says this:

First I will capture it
with nets traps helicopters dogs pieces
of string holes dug in the ground doped food
tranquilizer guns buckshot thrown stones
bows and arrows

Then I will name the species
after myself

. . . I will publish the results
in learned journals.

Which was the fate of the tiny Dawson caribou, an ice-age refugee that roamed the inland tundra of the Queen Charlotte Islands until 1910, when Matthew Yeomans and Henry White shot the last four of them ever seen alive, for the British Columbia Provincial Museum in Victoria. Which is what happened to the Fraser Valley that Marvin Rosenau knew when he was growing up, on the outskirts of Chilliwack, and as the years pass it is what happens to what he calls the "unique suite of genetically distinct organisms and microorganisms on each hillside." All the little sloughs were still there, and there were pheasants and skunks and coyotes. By the 1970s they had fallen to farm machinery and bulldozers.

In 1989, Canada Post was asking its letter carriers in Quebec City to refrain from throwing elastic bands into the sewer system because the few St. Lawrence River sturgeon that remain were becoming entangled in them.

Hydroelectric dams and water pollution and poachers that ran amok after the collapse of the Soviet Union had driven the giant Huso sturgeon from the Volga River and the Caspian Sea and the Sea of Azov, and the few that found refuge in the Liapin River were caught and cut up for caviar at the bureaucrats' congresses in Moscow.

In the spring of 1991, the first artificial spawning of sturgeon in Canadian history was accomplished at a federal fisheries hatchery at Inch Creek, near Mission. About 30,000 eggs were removed from a 60-pound female. The eggs were fertilized. Cell division occurred within hours. Fry emerged after 16 days.

In 1992 in northern Manitoba, provincial biologist Don Macdonald was working with the Cross Lake Indian Band to survey the rivers to see what was left of the lake sturgeon that were plentiful before hydro-electric dams, and were now facing extinction.

In 1993, biologists were combing the Alabama and Tombigbee rivers with gillnets, hoopnets, electric shock and rat poison hoping to find a fish that is suspected of being, or having been, a subspecies of the rare shovelnose sturgeon. They couldn't find one. No such fish had been seen in ten years.

In Israel, the first artificial caviar, a composite of flavours derived from the ground-up bits and pieces of various kinds of fish, has been developed at the Haifa Technion.

We take the obligatory photographs. The three of us are silent for a moment. Nick takes the fish by the tail in one hand and under the belly with the other and turns its head into the water. He holds it a moment, gently rocking it back and forth, letting water flow through its gills, until it is ready. It swims away.

It is swimming on the surface. It circles in the river, swims out and around, against the current. It comes back to the place where it had rested. It grounds on the shore at my feet.

It's confused, Nick says.

In Atwood's Oratorio, Man observes:

Now you have killed the god;
you have what you wanted.

Nick pulls the fish gently into the river again. It slaps its tail violently and swims quickly away.

She's fine, Nick says.

Atwood's Sasquatch survives, too. It is the man who is shot as he stumbles from the bush. Sasquatch calls the man his brother. From this occurrence, Sasquatch concludes:

. . . those who have destroyed you
will return in other bodies
to destroy me also;
already their saws, their axes
hack at my borders.

At nine in the morning on Sunday, August 21, 1994, a full year after the mysterious sturgeon deaths of 1993, a group of campers from Chilliwack's Island 22 campground found a ten-foot, 460-pound sturgeon washed up dead on a gravel bar near the mouth of the Harrison River. It was towed to the boat launch on the Chilliwack side of the river. Marvin Rosenau was there by 6 p.m.

Within a week, a dozen dead sturgeon, most of them old giants, had washed up on the banks of the river between Hope and Annacis Island. Within two weeks, the count was up to 21. The die-off was every bit as dramatic as the 1993 "event." Every possible cause was explored. All the same tests were run. The results turned up nothing.

On August 31, 1994, the Sto:lo Fisheries Authority banned all Native sturgeon fishing and imposed a mandatory live-release rule for all sturgeon caught in the tribal salmon fisheries. Most Sto:lo people were reluctant to eat sturgeon flesh because the river had become so polluted over the years, but the Sto:lo chiefs reckoned their initiative might make a difference. They challenged the provincial and federal governments to impose an immediate no-kill rule in the sturgeon sports fisheries and the commercial salmon fisheries.

The day the Sto:lo Fisheries Authority met to make the decision, Larry Commodore, who holds the environment portfolio for the Sto:lo Tribal Council, was standing in the corner of the room. He is the great-great-great-great-great grandson of Captain John, the Sto:lo leader who had argued a century earlier that the time had come "to enter protest against the wholesale slaughter of sturgeon in the Fraser River." On September 13, the challenge was met, and Marvin Rosenau's long-standing hopes for a shutdown of the sturgeon fisheries were realized. Federal fisheries minister Brian Tobin said it was imperative to act immediately to protect and conserve the white sturgeon. B.C. environment minister Moe Sihota expressed his sincere appreciation to the Sto:lo chiefs, and he called the new regulatory regime an excellent example of a unified response to a conservation problem.

The Sasquatch concludes the Oratorio:

We will go to the other country.
Under the mountains there is a sea,

it is summer here, there
it is winter. We will sit
together by that frozen shore

until the killers have been changed
to roots, to birds,

until the killers have become
the guardians and have learned
our language

waiting to be delivered
waiting to be made whole.

ACKNOWLEDGEMENTS AND SOURCES

First, Carl Leon.

Then Marvin Rosenau. Then George Brandak at the special collections library at the University of B.C., the staff at the Coqualeetza Archives at the Sto:lo Centre in Sardis, and Joss Halverson at the reference desk at the New Westminster Public Library.

The notion of citing Margaret Atwood's poem should be credited to the anthropologist Michael Ames, who juxtaposed Atwood's work with his reflections in the epilogue to the proceedings of a peculiar conference on the subject of cryptozoology, convened by the UBC Museum of Anthropology in 1978.

Portions of chapters three and four of this book have appeared in the *Georgia Straight*.

Documents gathered over several years contributed to the research for this book. In many instances, specific documents are cited in the text, but some useful sources were not. What follows should complete the list.

Ames, Michael and Marjorie Halpin, eds. *Manlike Monsters on Trial: Early Records and Modern Evidence*. University of British Columbia Press, Vancouver, 1980.

Atwood, Margaret. "Oratorio for Sasquatch, Man and Two Androids." In *Poems for Voices*, Canadian Broadcasting Corporation, Toronto, 1970.

Bohn, Glenn. "Sturgeon Most Recent Casualty of Rising Dioxin Contamination."

Vancouver *Sun*, November 29, 1990.

British Columbia, Ministry of the Environment, Department of Fisheries. "Lower Mainland Sturgeon Report," miscellaneous dates.

British Columbia, Ministry of the Environment, Department of Fisheries. Miscellaneous correspondence; annual reports; B.C. Fisheries Inspectors' Reports. Coqualeetza Archives and University of British Columbia special collections library.

Chilliwack *Progress*, April 26, 1905. Coqualeetza Archives

Duff, Wilson. "Field Notes," Notebook 3, 1950. Coqualeetza Archives

——. *The Upper Stalo Indians of the Fraser River of British Columbia*. Anthropology in British Columbia Memoir No. 1, British Columbia Provincial Museum, 1952.

"First Sturgeon Spawned in Canada." *Northern Aquaculture*, March–April, 1991.

"Fish Mystery: Where Do Adult Sturgeons Go?" Montreal *Gazette*, October 13, 1992.

Fladmark, Knut. *British Columbia Prehistory*. Archeological Survey of Canada, National Museum of Man, Ottawa, 1986.

Fraser, Simon. *The Letters and Journals of Simon Fraser*. W. Kaye Lamb, Editor. Macmillan and Company, Toronto, 1960.

Galbreath, Jim. "Columbia River Colossus — The White Sturgeon." *Oregon Wildlife*, March, 1979.

Georgia Straight, December 3–10, 1993.

Gibbard, John Edgar. "Early History of the Fraser Valley, 1808–1885." Master's thesis, Department of History, University of British Columbia, October, 1937.

Hartog, Diana. "Sturgeon." In *Polite to Bees*, Coach House Press, Toronto, 1992.

"Hydro Dams, Overfishing Could End Sturgeon's 65 Million Year History." Calgary *Herald*, May 10, 1992.

"Loch Research Suggests Nessie a Sturgeon." Montreal *Gazette*, January 22, 1994.

Lord, John Keast. *The Naturalist in Vancouver Island and British Columbia*. Richard Bentley, London, 1866.

Maud, Ralph, ed. *The Salish People: The Local Contributions of Charles Hill-Tout. Volume III — The Mainland Halkomelem*. Talonbooks, Vancouver, 1978.

Meggs, Geoff. *Salmon: The Decline of the British Columbia Fishery*. Douglas and McIntyre, Vancouver, 1991.

Mohs, Gordon. "The Upper Sto:lo Indians of British Columbia: An Ethno-Archeological Review." Heritage Consultants Report, Alliance of Tribal Councils, 1990.

——. "Spiritual Sites, Ethnic Significance and Native Spirituality: The Heritage and Heritage Sites of The Sto:lo Indians of British Columbia." Masters thesis,

Department of Archeology, Simon Fraser University, 1987.

——. "1990 Sto:lo Heritage Project, Final Report." Sto:lo Tribal Council, 1991.

New Westminster *Columbian* newspaper, July 11,1861; August 14, 1897. New Westminster Public Library, microfilm.

Northcote, T.G. "Biology of the Lower Fraser: A Review." Westwater Research Centre, University of British Columbia, Technical Report #3, n.d.

"Phantom Fish Story Alarms Alabama." Toronto *Globe and Mail*, November 23, 1993.

Richardson, Sir John. *Fauna Boreali-Americana; or The Zoology of the Northern Parts of British America, Part The Third, The Fish.* Richard Bentley, London, 1836.

Rosenau, Marvin. "White Sturgeon Concerns in the Lower Fraser River, A Discussion Document." B.C. Ministry of Environment, Lands and Parks, Victoria, 1993.

Scott, W.B. and E.J. Crossman, *Freshwater Fishes of Canada.* Fisheries Research Board of Canada, 1973.

Siemens, Alfred H. "The Lower Fraser Valley: Evolution of a Cultural Landscape." B.C. Geographical Series Number 9, Tantalus Research, Vancouver, 1966.

Sinclair, F.N. "A History of the Sumas Drainage, Dyking and Development District." Chilliwack Historical Society, 1961.

Smith, Theodore. "Culture of North American Sturgeons for Fishery Enhancement." South Carolina Marine Resources Center, n.d.

Stewart, Hilary. *Indian Fishing: Early Methods on the Northwest Coast.* J.J. Douglas, Vancouver, 1977.

"Sturgeon." *Seafood Business Magazine*, November–December, 1987.

Suttles, Wayne and Diamond Jenness. *Katzie Ethnographical Notes* and *The Faith of a Coast Salish Indian.* Wilson Duff, editor. Anthropology in British Columbia Memoirs Nos. 2 and 3, British Columbia Provincial Museum, 1955.

Thompson, Stith. *Motif-Index of Folk Literature.* Indiana University Press, Bloomington, Indiana, 1958.

Tower, W.S. "The Passing of the Sturgeon: A Case of the Unparalleled Extermination of a Species." *Popular Science Monthly*, 1909.

White, George B. "Development of the Eastern Fraser Valley." *B.C. Historical Quarterly*, October, 1948.

Please direct submissions and editorial enquiries to: Transmontanus, Box C-25, Fernhill Road, Mayne Island, B.C. V0N 2J0. All other correspondence, including sales and distribution enquiries, should be sent to New Star Books, 2504 York Avenue, Vancouver, B.C. V6K 1E3.

Publication of this book is made possible by grants from the Canada Council, the Canadian Heritage Book Publishing Industry Development Program, and the Cultural Services Branch, Province of British Columbia.

Series editor: Terry Glavin
Copy editor: Martin Dunphy
Design and production: Val Speidel
Cover photograph: Dan Hartlen
Map: Fiona MacGregor
Printed and bound in Canada by Best Book Manufacturers
1   2   3   4   5   98   97   96   95   94
First printing, November 1994

CATALOGUING IN PUBLICATION DATA

Glavin, Terry, 1955–
   A ghost in the water

   (Transmontanus, ISSN 1200-3336 ; 1)
   Includes bibliographic references.
   ISBN 0-921586-38-8

   1. Sturgeons – British Columbia – Fraser River. 2.
Sturgeons – Folklore. I. Title. II. Series.
QL638.A25G62   1994   597'.44   C94-910943-6

A strange prehistoric giant, rarely seen and little understood, haunts the depths of the Fraser River. It is the Fraser River white sturgeon, the largest freshwater fish in North America, and it is facing extinction. *A Ghost in the Water* is about the sturgeon and its ancient relationship with the people who live in the river valley.

A Ghost in the Water is the first book in the series *Transmontanus*, which explores the relationship between people and the landscape in what has come to be known as British Columbia.

Terry Glavin is the author of *A Death Feast in Dimlahamid* and *Nemiah: The Unconquered Country.*

$12

ISSN 1200-3336

ISBN 0-921586-38-8

9 780921 586395

Published by New Star Books